AF230917

'First, find out what your hero wants, then just follow him!'

Ray Bradbury

published by Bluebudgie Publishing
ISBN: 978-0-9568666-4-6
© L.Murphy 2013
Printed by Createspace, Charleston SC.
USA.
First edition.

THE SPRING BOARD BOOK

by

LORNA MURPHY

THE SPRINGBOARD BOOK

There are no stories in this book.

They are still in your head.

All the characters in these pictures are waiting for you to tell their stories.

There is some text you can use as hints to the untold tale, or you can completely ignore them and go your own way.

If you get stuck, look at the pictures and ask questions. Lots of them.

- What's going on here?

- What's her name?

- What is he doing?

- How did they get there?

- Where are they?

You get the idea.. or hopefully you *will* get loads of them!
And before you know it, the whole story will appear on your page.

So pen and paper ready? Then come on inside.
They're waiting...

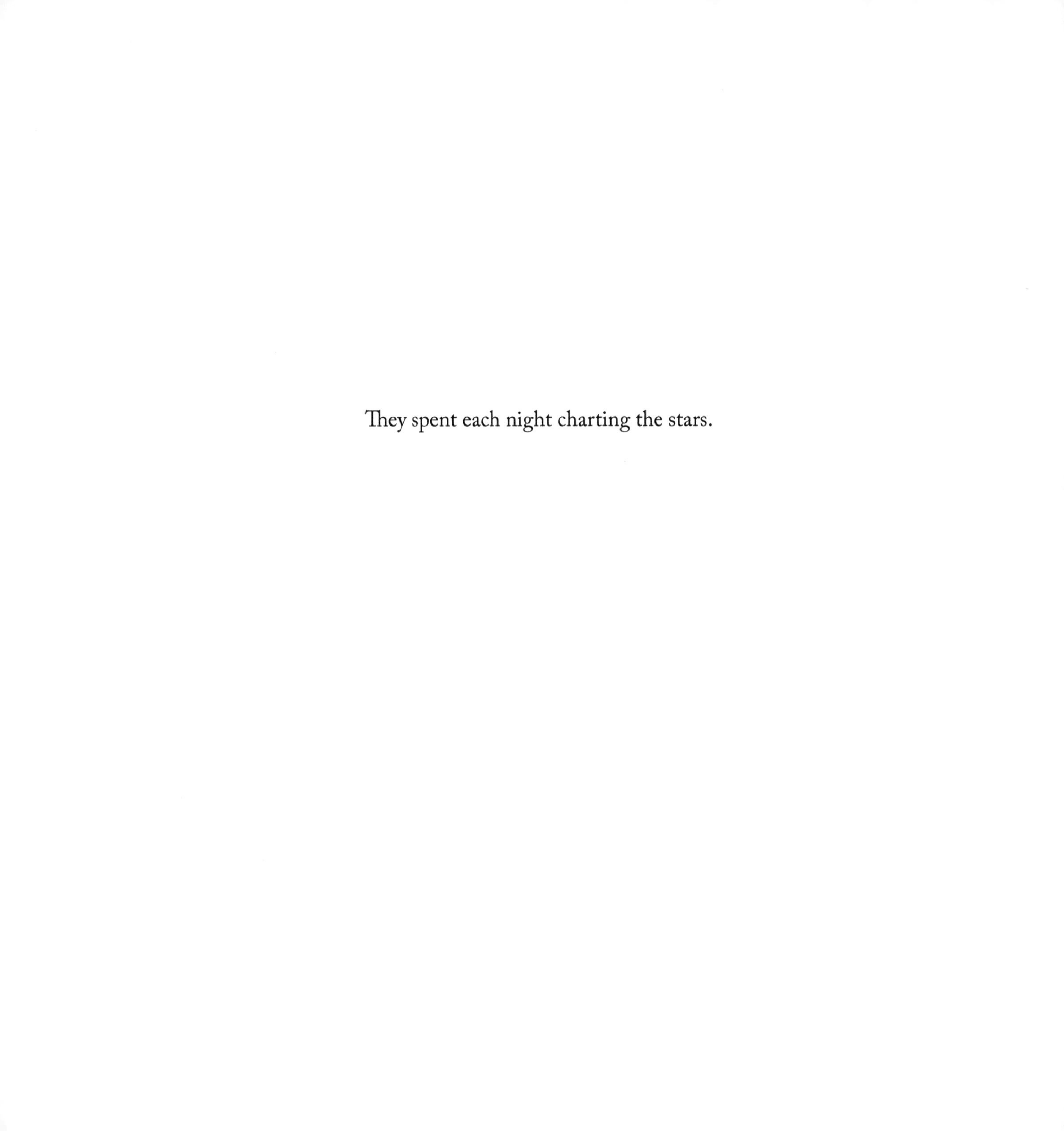

They spent each night charting the stars.

STAR CHART

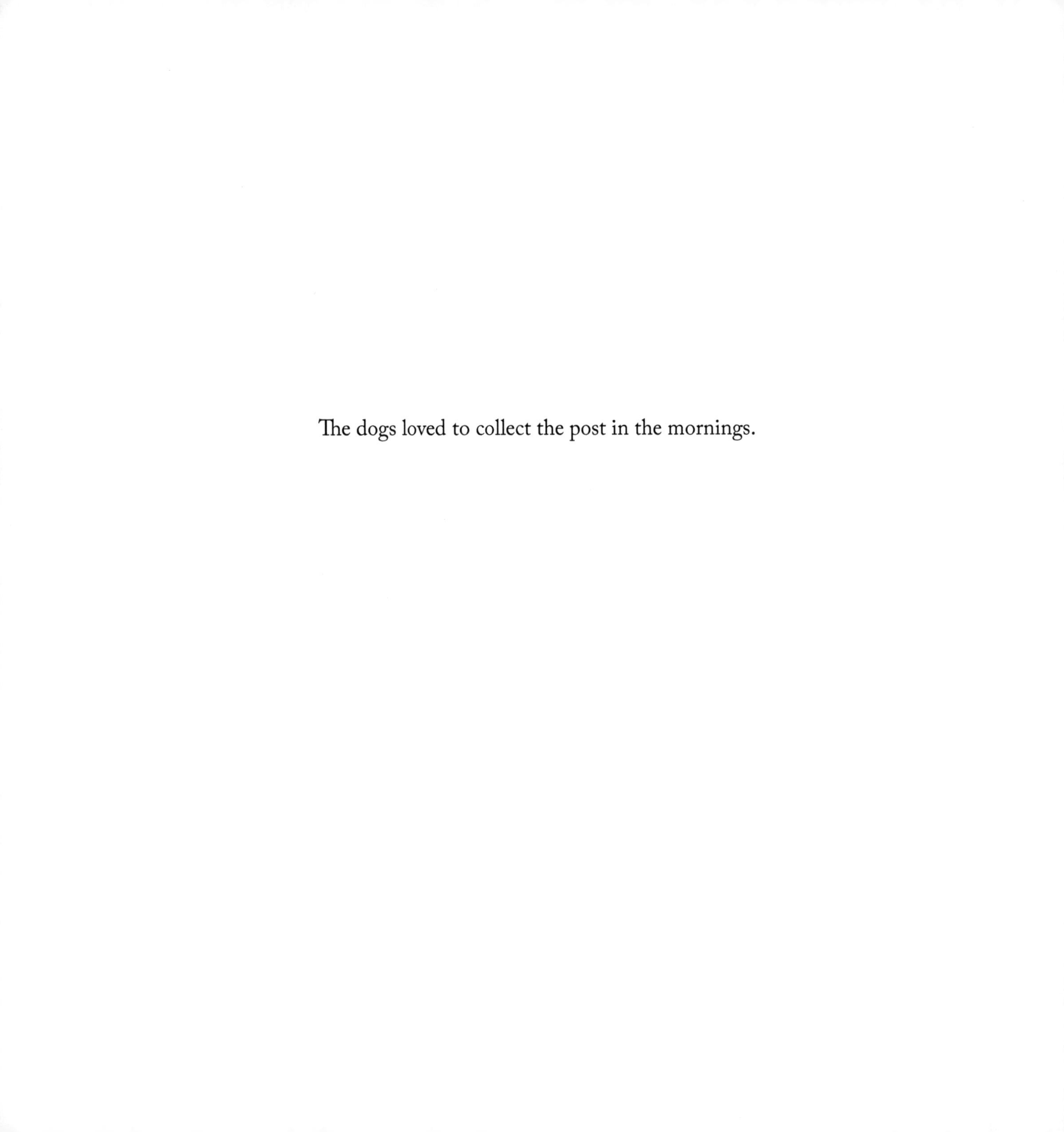

The dogs loved to collect the post in the mornings.

OPO

I asked Dr. Fenster why one of his windows was blacked out.

"I don't like the view from there" he replied.

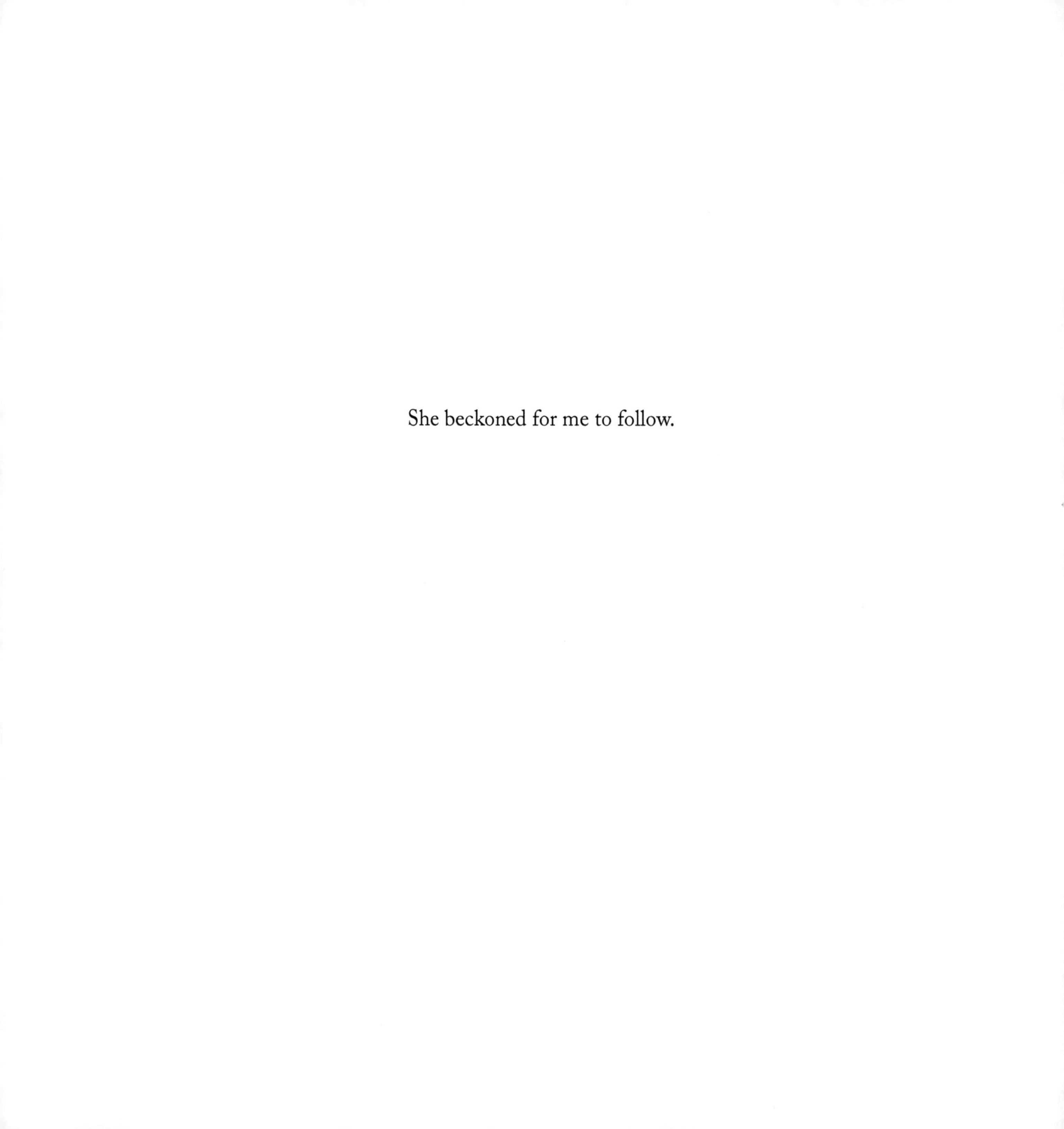

She beckoned for me to follow.

The huge blast blew out the cheese walls and they lost no time escaping.

Danny just smiled.

THE END

DUSK BUSES.

42
20
5
13
13
43
DUSK BUSSTOP
3

Time never quite caught up with Francois, so he lived young and for a very
long time.

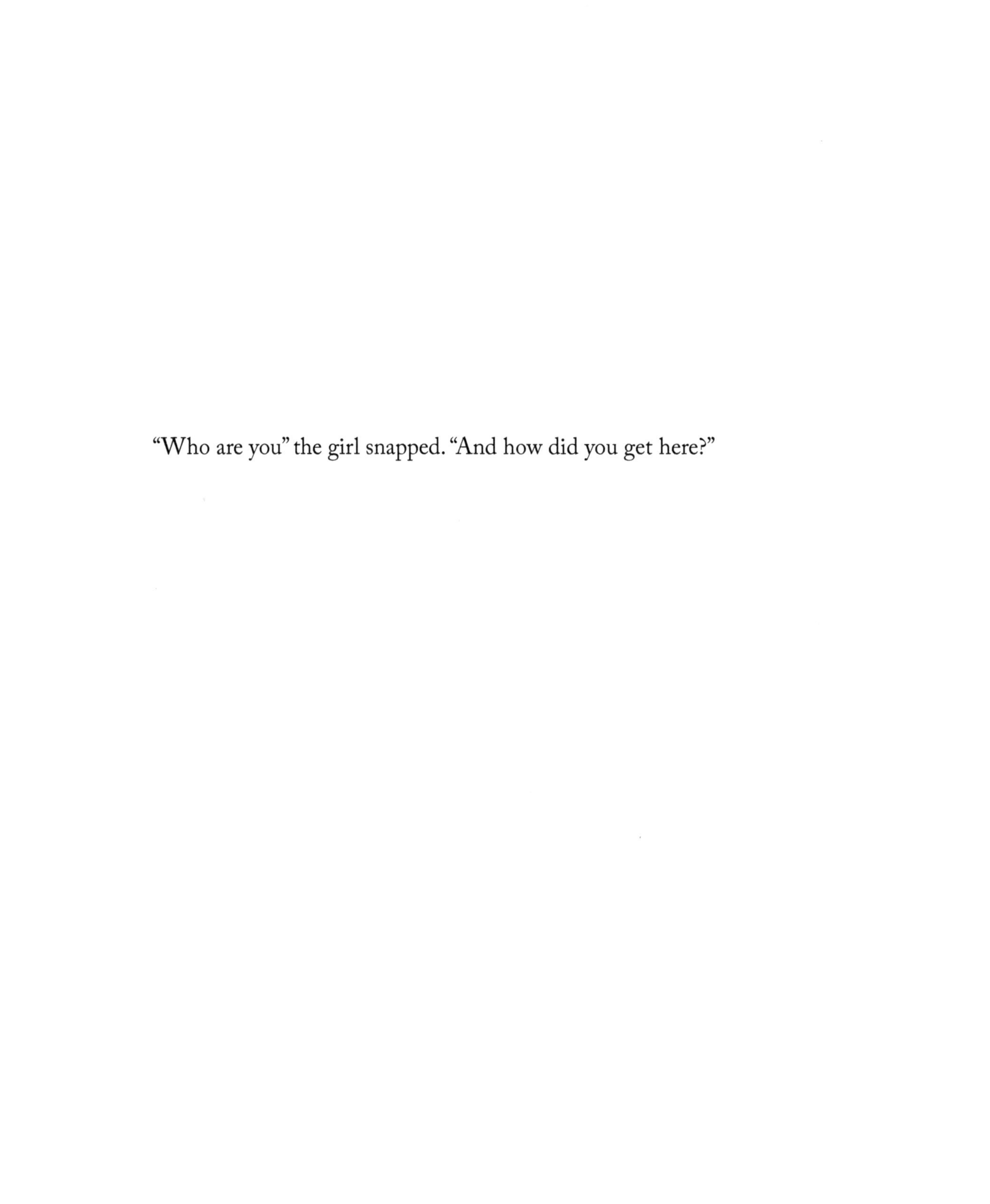

“Who are you” the girl snapped. “And how did you get here?”

MICHAEL JACKSON'S GLOVE

He would give anything to have that glove and slip it on to his useless hand. That night he decided to steal it.

At precisely 1 p.m. London Time, every dolphin in the ocean began to head west and everybody knew that the world was about to change forever.

I hope you found something to inspire you in this book.

So what now?

Why not bring your stories along to school, college or writing class or submit it to a competition? Or if you're not feeling quite ready to share, just keep it under your bed to re-read yourself when you feel like it.

Don't worry if you think something hasn't quite worked, the key thing is NOT to give up. Keep everything. As long as you keep writing and creating you'll get better - and you'll be able to look back at these stories to see how far you've come.

If you would like to send me your stories. I will be setting up a website to post them on and will email you as soon as it is up and running , or if you want to tell me how the pictures inspired you, I would love to hear from you.

Here is the address: **lornamurph23@gmail.com**

Happy storytelling!

Till next time.

Lorna Murphy

BLUEBUDGIE

www.ingramcontent.com/pod-product-compliance
Lightning Source LLC
Chambersburg PA
CBHW042157030726
47599CB00004B/766